Transform Yourself and Change your Life:

KEYS TO AN ABUNDANT LIFE

Marie H Jean-Louis

ISBN: 978-1-7343554-0-6
ISBN: 978-1-7343554-1-3 (e)

Contact information: Mariehjeanlouis3@gmail.com
Printed in the United States of America

Because of the dynamic nature of the internet, any web addresses or links contained in this book may have changed since publication and may no longer be valid.

The intent of the author is only to offer information of a general nature to help you in your quest for emotional and spiritual well-being. They are not to be understood as directions, recommendations, or prescriptions of any kind.

If you choose to use any of the information in this book for yourself, the author and publisher assume no responsibility for your actions.

Other products by Marie H Jean-Louis include:
Light of Love poetry book

ABOUT THE AUTHOR

Marie H Jean-Louis is an Advanced Registered Nurse Practitioner with a doctoral degree in Nursing Practice and a certification in education. She is a Healing Touch student and a member of the Healing Touch Professional Association. She enjoys volunteering her time to help others. Marie studied nursing with the purpose of helping people and changing lives. She spent years providing physical, emotional, and spiritual care to patients. The art of teaching and listening has enabled her to connect at a deeper spiritual level with her patients. Many patients told her how her positive words of inspiration, love, and motivation have helped them change their lives. She made it her goal to reach a wider audience through her book with a focus for enlightenment, love, and transformation. She is the author of a published poetry book *Light of Love*.

ACKNOWLEDGMENTS

I thank all of you who in one way or another have helped me become who I AM today. It is because of those experiences and guidance that this book is made available to you.

I thank you for letting me be part of your journey

To my family, Oscar and Sassy: I love you

$\mathcal{T}$ABLE OF CONTENTS

PREFACE

It was with great pleasure that I wrote this book to enlighten people and help bring spiritual awareness. It is not intended to dictate how to live your lives or your spirituality. Let it serve as a guide in helping you find your path in life. I am grateful to be in service and be a voice, an instrument, in helping you make changes in your life. My infinite gratitude to God for its EVERLASTING DIVINE LOVE and for using me as an instrument to help others.

In love and gratitude,

Dr. Marie H Jean-Louis

LOVE ME INSIDE OUT

I look in the mirror
I see a stranger
My body I no longer recognize
My smile I lost in my misery
I look for love, but it seems nonexistent
My body cries for life
Alone I sit in a corner, hungry for love
Wondering if you hear me
I am lost
Show me the way
Guide me to the river of life
The source of everlasting love
For my soul to be alive
And my brightness to shine

ƒNTRODUCTION

I say Yes! Yes! Yes! to the universe.

Those were the words I shouted after I started on my healing journey. I embarked on this holistic healing after experiencing disappointments, heartaches, and frustrations in certain areas of my life. My unhappiness prompted me to question life. For example, why wasn't I successful in achieving everything that I desired in my life? That question opened the door to a quest for spirituality and truth. At that time, I did not know that quest would take me on a journey that would transform me and my life significantly.

The spiritual journey to me is like a puzzle where I have to constantly create my life and evolve based on the choices that I make. Throughout my life, I made choices and knocked on doors that did not yield the best experiences. Nevertheless, I still had to deal with those unpleasant experiences and I learned from them. After a while, I finally understood that no matter which door one choses to knock on or enter, there is always an experience to learn from. The key is for you to choose which experience you want to create, for once you learn that, your life will transform in an inexplicable way. You will enter into the pure essence of who you really are: Love and Light. Then your quest will be over, for you will know that you have reached HOME.

In my journey, I had to learn to let go of what no longer served me and focus on God/Source or whatever way you refer to Him. I had to unlearn what I taught was truth in order to learn the real truth, my truth. Letting go of old beliefs was a challenge for me because they were so ingrained in my mind. I had to change my perceptions and beliefs to see myself in a totally different way: a beautiful spiritual being, made in the likeness of God, having a human experience. Therefore, as an extension of God/Source, I am powerful, magnificent, worthy, limitless, and can have everything that I desire. It is a transformation that takes time, dedication, and work. As I mentioned above, it is a journey.

I learned to honor and forgive myself and others, not only for things done to me but also for things I have done to myself and to others. I was still seeking answers and asking questions until one day I found love hidden right inside of me. Not realizing how powerful it was going to make me, I found myself surrendering to this magnificent being within me, GOD. In the process, I have come to remember who I truly AM, learned to love myself, and experienced unconditional love. Know now that you have all it takes within you to succeed and have whatever you desire in life. Trust in God and His power.

My truth to you is to learn to love yourself and the God within you. Meditation is a great tool to help you experience that divine love. Once experienced, it is the greatest love of all. You can't love another until you love yourself first. Neither can you have abundance until you remember who you truly are. As stated in the Bible, "Seek ye first the Kingdom of God, then all things will be added unto you" (Matthew 6:33 KJV). I discovered the keys to an abundant life is to first seek and acknowledge the God within you, second to practice love especially self-love and gratitude, third to honor God and yourself and finally to have peace and happiness.

This is my journey. I encourage you to follow your heart and find your truth.

KNOW YOUR WORTH

Dear One,

All is not over! Life does not end just because he left you. Just like you existed before you knew him, you will continue to exist after him. Brace yourself, wipe your tears, for deliverance is coming to you soon. You will see the sun rises, the brightness of the stars and the moonlight. Life was not meant to always be without challenges but for us to find our peace within them. What may seem impossible to you now may be your strength tomorrow. Remember you are not alone. God is always with you.

Wake up from your sadness and sorrow, tomorrow will be better. Solitude is needed in order to remember who you are and help you in life. Rejoice that you have overcome and become stronger. Nothing is meant to last forever as we are constantly evolving. Learn to love yourself and others and surrender to the force, the power that is within you. Many have sought love in the wrong places and ended up with heartaches. Seek love not from the outside but from within. No matter how much you try to ignore that part of you, it will always be there waiting for you. Know yourself, speak love and truth. Inspire others to do the same regardless of the situation.

I NEED YOU

Don't leave me alone
The pain is too much to bear
Stay with me
I need your strength to know that I will make it through
Help me! Fear is coming upon me
I need to feel you and hold you
To touch your presence
Suddenly I feel alone on this endless road
With no help, no sounds from the wind or the birds
Wondering how I am going to make it alone
I feel weak
Help me! Give me your hand
Tell me that all will be all right
For I can't make it alone
I desperately need you
Give me the courage of a warrior
The strength of a lion
The power of the universe
And a faith that is unwavering
For in you I trust, GOD

HOPE

Look past the horizon, for there lies a vibrant tomorrow
There lies hope and inspiration
Reach for the stars
Knowing that there is no limitation
Dream of the impossible
For it is attainable
Trust in your abilities and divinity
For you will soon realize your power

YOU TOO ARE LOVED

No matter your faith
Know that you are loved by God
You have a purpose here on earth
Seek it
Once revealed
Watch your life change
and joy be your new song
Live life a moment at a time
so miracles don't escape you
Enjoy yourself, have fun
Love, laugh
Honor yourself, your sexuality
Your uniqueness, your authenticity
Honor your power, your wisdom
Honor life
Honor your magnificence
Honor GOD

GRATITUDE

Magnificent I AM, oh! GOD
I AM grateful for such splendor
Worthy I AM
So precious and powerful
I AM much more than what the mirror reveals to me
I AM vibrant
Vibrating love, peace, and joy all around me
For I was made in your likeness, oh GOD

LOVE

People perceive love differently. I choose to write about it because, as human beings, this is what our souls were created for. Our journey here on earth is to experience love and share it. Unfortunately, many of us will spend our lifetime never really experiencing true divine love. It is all around us, but, unless we start seeing with our hearts, we may never experience it. Not long ago, I was talking to someone who experienced a heart break from a romantic relationship. She was devastated, trying to understand how love could have betrayed her, caused her pain, and given her all these negative feelings and emotions. The reason is because the love some of us share is conditional. Therefore, when the conditions are not in our favor, we change. We start acting and creating negative feelings and emotions, not only within us but also towards others as well. So let's change our perception of love.

You see, conditional love is never fulfilling. You are always looking for something outside of yourself to please you and give you joy. That is depending on something or someone to help fulfill that void within you. And the joy you experience is always short-lived because it is superficial. But once you discover your passion, that which fulfills your soul, that joy is permanent, eternal. As far as relationships go, the first should be with yourself, fulfilling your soul's needs. It is by achieving soul fulfillment that you will be successful in any relationship.

For the goal of any relationship is to help each other evolve while knowing that each of you is a complete being.

I believe that understanding of spirituality makes loving another human being easier because you realize that we are all made from that one universal energy and consciousness. We all are from source and have God/source energy within us. Therefore, that person you passed in the street is a reflection of the magnificent light energy that is within you and vice versa. Spiritually speaking, this is who we are. However, our negative human habits and our ego sometimes prevent that light from shining. Once you learn self- love, then you can love another being, for, what you would want for yourself, you would want for the other person as well.

THE POWER OF LOVE

Love has captured me and pulled me out of this place of
sorrow
Love has opened me up to life
Love has freed me up from prison
Love delivered me from pain
I am now healed, rescued by the hands of love
Feeling the vibration of love, I am my divine self
It is this melody caressing my body and taking me to unusual
places
It is the power of my soul
The sensual part of me
It is my nature

TO AN AMAZING MAN

To my husband, never underestimate my love for you
Not like anything you have ever experienced before
I dreamt of you before I even met you
I waited many seasons to meet you
Allow me to nurture you
Heal your wounds
Carry your offspring
My love for you is rooted so deep
Allow me to raise your vibration to this secret mysterious
realm
Hear me now, come closer
Take my hand, hold me tight
Nothing else exists but you and me

EXPRESSION OF LOVE

My love, no one can take me away from you
Loving you, loving me is perfect
Feeling your vibration even when I am not with you
Know thee that I cherish you
I cleanse myself in order to experience your magic
Standing naked before you, my cells scream of joy
Manifesting you was my biggest pleasure
Loving you is my soul purpose

LOVE YOU NO MATTER WHAT

Turning my life around
So I can love you
Hear you sing
Come with me to our secret place
for a mesmerizing adventure
Let me help you discover ecstasy
Love changed me, healed me
Let my love transform you
No matter where you go I am with you
My intention is to always be with you
Cease to run away from love
Look into my eyes to see the fire of my love
Don't run away
My passion and kindness are enough
Return home
Where your soul vibrates to its true essence

SELF-LOVE

Self-love is unfamiliar to most people. Many would argue that they love themselves because they don't cause self-harm. Self-love goes deeper than the physical. It is the thoughts you think of yourself, the things you do to honor yourself, the kindness you show to yourself, the acceptance of yourself, the way you carry yourself, the joy you bring into your life, your authenticity and truth in two words: self-care. How many times have you told yourself, "I love you?" How many times have you hugged yourself? How many times have you honored your feelings? For many of us the answers to these questions may be never.

We live in such a busy world that is always demanding more of us and at an excessive speed. So, in return, we forget and neglect ourselves. And some of us don't even know how to care for and nurture ourselves. Just like there are different seasons, moonlight and daylight in the universe, so our bodies also have cycles. Our bodies require time to be active, passive, to have fun, relax, be pampered, and meditate. Listen to your body and honor those feelings. You can start by taking just 5 or 10 minutes a day from your busy schedule to do something that you enjoy.

It could be a walk in the park, listening to your favorite music, taking a nap, meditating or sitting in silence. Make that time a daily rendezvous with yourself. As you progress, you can increase the duration and incorporate other activities that you enjoy in your schedule. Book that trip that you always wanted. Why? Because it will bring you joy and you are worth it. Another good practice is to tell yourself "I love you" every day. It may feel strange at first, but as you continue you will feel comfortable. As you do these activities, watch how your body reacts to them. Listen to your intuition and feel what sensations come up and honor them.

We often ask people, what is your passion? Some of them don't even know. But when you ask them what is it that makes you happy, laugh, the thing that you enjoy doing or hearing all day without being tired? They usually are able to relate. I believe that every one of us has that spark in us that brings us joy. The universe intended for it to be that way to help bring us home. Don't try to resist it.

AWAKEN

Uncertainty is what I feel when you are away
No longer will I mourn your absence
For I discover my own wisdom
Beneath it all was this treasure of life
Seek not after your empty treasure for the temporary plea-
sures it can offer
I sit and swim in a pool of water that serves as my mirror
No one bothers to look at me, for I am unfamiliar
But vast and deep I AM
My roots are anchored deep and deep
I birth what you need to achieve greatness
If you were to close your eyes, you would see my sanctuary
You would speak with your mouth yet close
Step foot in my sanctuary and be transformed

PROUD TO BE ME

I walk with my head up high
My hair braided down to my shoulders
My chest forward reveals an ample bosom
As I walk I swing my hips with each step
A desirable posterior
complements my physique
I smile to those stopping to look at me
And to those that follow
I say, know that you are magnificent

LOVING ME UNCONDITIONALLY

I wake up this morning loving me
Loving every part of my being
The freckles on my face
The shape of my nose
The size of hips
The scars on my body
Loving my sexuality
And accepting who I AM
I love being me
The way I smile, talk, laugh
I love me unconditionally

PHENOMENAL YOU ARE

I love you, your morning smile
Like the sunrise in my somber day
your sweetness I long for
For it is nourishment to my hunger
I love me
Not because of you loving me
Because I know who I AM
I know my worth
I love me
Not because of you loving me
Because I honor myself
And know that I AM phenomenal

SPLENDID

Your beauty woke me up from my deep sleep
I wonder if you even noticed
My dear, I am my own admirer
What I possess, I cherish
There was a time I was blind, lost, and ignorant
Love has found me
Transformed me
So that I can stand in my magnificence

WORDS OF WISDOM

Love who you have become in this transformational process of your life. Wisdom comes with knowledge and experience. Those experiences joyful or painful were necessary to help you become who you are today. Be grateful for them and the people in your life especially those who have pushed your buttons. We are each other's teachers striving to reach our highest potential. None of us is superior than the other, we are all created equal. Life was not meant to be difficult but experiential and fun if we were to follow our intuition. The goal is for you to find peace and love in the midst of chaos.

Everyone's journey is different, so there is no need for comparison. Each one of us will achieve our goals at our perfect time. It is a process that cannot be rushed. It is perfectly designed by the Universe.

Enjoy your journey!

HURRY

Hurry, hurry!

The time is now to reveal your masterpiece

You have consumed unimaginable fuel

Devoted countless seasons to your precious masterpiece

Eager are we to experience and live your story

carefully chiseling the parts that no longer fit

Know that, what you are yearning for, you already are

Waste no more time!

Working through Dawn and night seeing only daylight

Challenging it is! For your conception is to create perfection

Perhaps your eyes keep deceiving you each time

Now our curiosity is at rest

Your masterpiece finally revealed

And ouch! How magnificent it is

It's you. This masterpiece is a reflection of you

Dear one, remove the veils obstructing the true vision of

who you are

See that you were perfect all along

SACRED

You need silence for the wisdom of God to come through
Just like water cascading from a waterfall, it is powerful,
flawless, and beautiful
The vibration is like nothing felt before
Powerful enough to clear or heal any imperfections
fulfill all needs
It is a state of all knowing
A place of magnificence
Love
Endless possibilities
A place of wisdom
Allow yourself to experience the bliss

A SOUL CONNECTION

"Come in! The door is open," I say.

As he walks through the door, my smile brightens. Seeing his perfect silhouette and his charm always awakens my core senses. The smile cannot disappear from my face as I offer him a seat.

"Anything to drink?" I ask.

"Tea," he replies. He adds, "Unsweetened, please."

Without much delay, I bring two cups of unsweetened green tea and place them on the coffee table. I already know that green tea is his favorite. I sit next to him on the couch. We both sip the tea and enjoy its aroma and natural sweetness.

We are silent, but yet we are communicating. There is this magnetic force, pulling us closer towards each other. We both feel the connection, the desire, and the passion. For an instant, our eyes meet and lock. Then only the two of us exist as we succumb to this beautiful, magical moment. We are no longer two but one. As we enjoy each other's body, each movement, touch, and sound we make, reflecting a deeper connection. Our eyes meet again, drawing our souls together. There is a feeling of bliss, beauty, oneness, perfection, love, and acceptance. It is a feeling, a sensation never felt before as we surrender and explode in joy.

We both know that what we share is deeper than we are and we cannot even comprehend it. We cuddle and often feel the energy flowing through our bodies, causing a snapping or jerking reaction. We laugh, kiss, and allow ourselves to relive this magical experience over and over again. We want to stay in this unimaginable place forever.

As we continue our journey, that day and those moments will be registered in our memories forever. How could love be so strong? There are no dimensions or ways to measure true love. Three years later we sit on a bench in a park watching our three-year-old girl play while we are reminiscing about that magical day. We look at each other with deep love and admiration as we smile.

This is an experience that we will share with her at the perfect time. As for us, we are still living life to its fullest, creating magical memories every day and every step of the way.

MYSTERY REVEALED

Love me not for who you think I am
I change with the seasons on earth
and share sunset and sunrise with the universe
I bear fruits and enjoy my diversity
Nothing escapes me
My desires I always fulfill
I remain dormant no longer
I was forgotten and lonely
Until I was out of my dream
Awake now, I remember my origin
Blessings and love I share
Creation I delight in
Experiences I long for
My purpose is to fully express who I AM
Divinity

Thank you for letting me be part of your journey
In love and gratitude,

Dr. Marie H. Jean-Louis

DAILY
INSPIRATIONAL
WORDS

POWER

TRUTH

TRUST

PATIENCE

PEACE

INTEGRITY

WISDOM

PATIENCE

SELF LOVE

SELF WORTH

HARMONY

HEALING

HEALTH

PROSPERITY

HONESTY

JOY

KINDNESS

FAITH

INSPIRATION

EMPOWERMENT

DREAM

ABUNDANCE

ENLIGHTENMENT

RESPECT

TRANSFORMATION

LAUGHTER

DIVERSITY

FREEDOM

HONOR

MASTERY

FORGIVENESS

COURAGE

CONFIDENCE

SUCCESS

GRATITUDE

DELIVERANCE

THANK YOU

REFLECTIONS

www.ingramcontent.com/pod-product-compliance
Lightning Source LLC
Chambersburg PA
CBHW021506090426

42739CB00007B/496